IN OUR CLASSROOM

HOW WE LEARN AND PLAY IN OUR OWN WAY

In Our Classroom helps empower students by teaching them to think about what is just right for them, celebrate their differences, and embrace one another to build an inclusive classroom community.

This book is dedicated to all the children I have taught throughout the years. Thank you for helping me learn how to teach in a way that is "just right" for everyone.

Each year, a group of children and a teacher come together to form a class.

Our class becomes a little community of learners for the year.

Each student in our class is unique and special.

We can communicate in different ways.

We can move our bodies using our legs, wheels, or other equipment.

We learn in different ways too!

Some students learn best on a computer.

Some students will work with different teachers.

Some students learn while using buttons, pictures, or a device.

Some students learn while sitting in a specific chair.

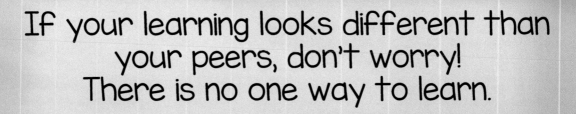

If your learning looks different than your peers, don't worry!
There is no one way to learn.

As we learn, we worry about ourselves and what is just right for us and our own learning.

We listen to each other.

We use nice words and are kind to each other.

We share.

We learn about each other.

We support each other.

We look out for each other.

We stand up for one another.

We cheer each other on.

22

We include each other
as we learn and play.

In our classroom, we are here for each other every step of the way!

24

78904254R00017

Empowering students to focus on what is just right for them, celebrate their differences, and embrace one another to build an inclusive classroom community.

ISBN 9798839236363

BASEBALL

BELONGING

Written by **Ryan Lavarnway**

World Series Champion & Olympian

Illustrated by **Chris Brown**

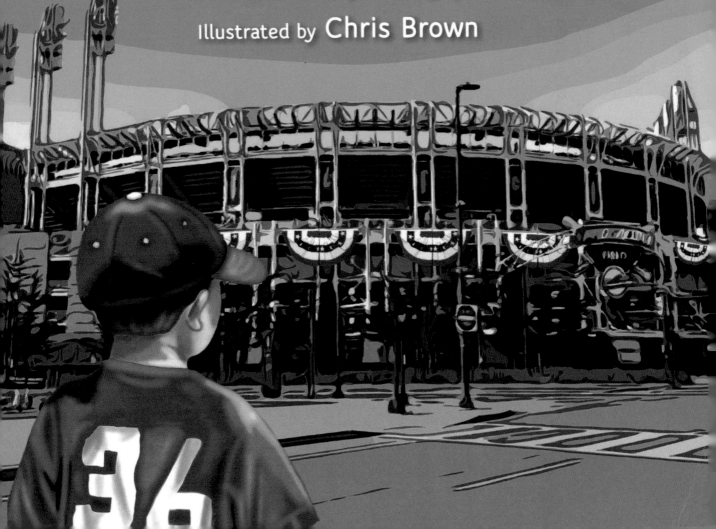